To

_____

From

_____

Date

_____

C000228482

Previously published under the title
199 Favorite Bible Verses for Busy Moms

© 2010 Christian Art Gifts Inc., IL, USA
      Christian Art Publishers, RSA

First edition 2010
Second edition 2019

Designed by Christian Art Publishers

Images used under license from Shutterstock.com

Scripture quotations marked NIV are taken from the *Holy Bible*,
New International Version® NIV®. Copyright © 1973, 1978, 1984
by International Bible Society. Used by permission of Zondervan
Publishing House. All rights reserved.

Scripture quotations marked NLT are taken from the *Holy Bible*, New
Living Translation®, second edition. Copyright © 1996, 2004 by Tyndale
House Publishers, Inc., Carol Stream, Illinois 60188. All rights reserved.

Scripture quotations marked THE MESSAGE are taken from *The Message*.
Copyright © by Eugene H. Peterson, 1993, 1994, 1995. Used by
permission of NavPress Publishing Group.

Scripture quotations marked ESV are taken from the *Holy Bible*, English
Standard Version, copyright © 2001 by Crossway Bibles, a division of
Good News Publishers. Used by permission. All rights reserved.

Scripture quotations marked NCV are taken from the *Holy Bible*,
New Century Version®. Copyright © 1987, 1988, 1991, 2005 by Word
Publishing, a division of Thomas Nelson, Inc. Used by permission.

Printed in China

ISBN 978-1-4321-3080-0

© All rights reserved. No part of this book may be reproduced in any
form without permission in writing from the publisher, except in the
case of brief quotations embodied in critical articles or reviews.

19 20 21 22 23 24 25 26 27 28 – 10 9 8 7 6 5 4 3 2 1

199
FAVORITE
BIBLE VERSES
for *Mothers*

**CHRISTIAN ART
PUBLISHERS**

CONTENTS

Wake Up Call

Scripture to Help You
Start the Day Right

*I still find each day too short
for all the thoughts I want to think,
all the walks I want to take, all the
books I want to read and all the
friends I want to see.*

John Burroughs

*When you feel like
giving up, remember why
you held on for so long in
the first place.*

Anonymous

Wake Up Call
Encouragement

1

The LORD your God is in your midst,
a mighty One who will save;
He will rejoice over you with gladness;
He will quiet you by His love;
He will exult over you with loud singing.

Zephaniah 3:17 ESV

2

The faithful love of the LORD never ends!
His mercies never cease. Great is
His faithfulness; His mercies begin
afresh each morning.

Lamentations 3:22-23 NLT

3

"Not by might nor by power, but
by My Spirit," says the LORD Almighty.

Zechariah 4:6 NIV

4

Delight yourself in the LORD and He will give you the desires of your heart.

Psalm 37:4 NIV

5

May our Lord Jesus Christ Himself, who loved us and by His grace gave us eternal encouragement and good hope, encourage your hearts and strengthen you in every good deed and word.

2 Thessalonians 2:16-17 NIV

6

Blessings crown the head of the righteous.

Proverbs 10:6 NIV

7

The Scriptures give us hope and
encouragement as we wait patiently
for God's promises to be fulfilled.

Romans 15:4 NLT

*Instead of giving myself
reasons why I can't; I give
myself reasons why I can.*

Anonymous

*At times our own light
goes out and is rekindled
by a spark from another
person. Each of us has cause
to think with deep gratitude
of those who have lighted
the flame within us.*

Albert Schweitzer

Wake Up Call
Gratitude

8

Since everything God created is
good, we should not reject any
of it, but receive it with thanks.

1 Timothy 4:4 NLT

9

Be joyful always, pray continually,
give thanks in all circumstances;
for this is God's will for you
in Christ Jesus.

1 Thessalonians 5:16-18 NIV

10

I will give thanks to the LORD
with my whole heart; I will recount
all of Your wonderful deeds.

Psalm 9:1 ESV

11

Let your roots grow down into Him,
and let your lives be built on Him.
Then your faith will grow strong in the
truth you were taught, and you will
overflow with thankfulness.

Colossians 2:7 NLT

12

The LORD is good and His love
endures forever; His faithfulness
continues through all generations.

Psalm 100:5 NIV

13

Light is shed upon the righteous
and joy on the upright in heart.

Psalm 97:11 NIV

14

No eye has seen, no ear has heard, and no mind has imagined what God has prepared for those who love Him.

1 Corinthians 2:9 NLT

15

A cheerful heart fills the day with song.

Proverbs 15:15 THE MESSAGE

*May your walls know joy;
may every room hold
laughter and every window
open to great possibility.*

Maryanne Radmacher-Hershey

Wake Up Call

Joy

16

This is the day the LORD has made;
let us rejoice and be glad in it.

Psalm 118:24 NIV

17

In Him our hearts rejoice,
for we trust in His holy name.

Psalm 33:21 NLT

18

I am overwhelmed with joy
in the LORD my God!

Isaiah 61:10 NLT

19

The joy of the LORD is your strength.

Nehemiah 8:10 ESV

20

Let all who take refuge in You be glad;
let them ever sing for joy. Spread Your
protection over them, that those who
love Your name may rejoice in You.

Psalm 5:11 NIV

21

Satisfy us in the morning with Your
steadfast love, that we may rejoice and
be glad all our days.

Psalm 90:14 ESV

22

I know the LORD is always
with me. No wonder my heart
is glad, and I rejoice.

Psalm 16:8-9 NLT

23

Rejoice in the Lord always.

Philippians 4:4 NIV

24

The Holy Spirit produces this kind of
fruit in our lives: joy.

Galatians 5:22 NLT

Joy is the echo of God's
life within us.

Joseph Marmion

*The greatest part
of our happiness
depends on our dispositions,
not our circumstances.*

Martha Washington

Is this Really My Life?

Scripture to Help You
Get through the Day

The sun can break through the darkest cloud; love can brighten the gloomiest day.

William Arthur Ward

Is this Really My Life?
Comfort

25

May Your unfailing love be my
comfort, according to Your promise
to Your servant.

Psalm 119:76 NIV

26

The more we suffer for Christ,
the more God will shower us with
His comfort through Christ.

2 Corinthians 1:5 NLT

27

If your heart is broken, you'll find GOD
right there; if you're kicked in the gut,
He'll help you catch your breath.

Psalm 34:18 THE MESSAGE

28

"As a mother comforts her child,
so will I comfort you."

Isaiah 66:13 NIV

29

Those who plant in tears will harvest
with shouts of joy.

Psalm 126:5 NLT

30

God heals the brokenhearted
and binds up their wounds.

Psalm 147:3 NIV

31

Weeping may last through the night,
but joy comes with the morning.

Psalm 30:5 NLT

32

"I'll be with you, day after day after
day, right up to the end of the age."

Matthew 28:20 THE MESSAGE

*In Christ the heart of the Father
is revealed, and higher comfort
there cannot be than to rest
in the Father's heart.*

Andrew Murray

*Endurance is not
just the ability to
bear a hard thing,
but to turn it
into glory.*

William Barclay

Is this Really My Life?
Endurance

33

You need to persevere so that when you have done the will of God, you will receive what He has promised.

Hebrews 10:36 NIV

34

Let us not grow weary of doing good, for in due season we will reap, if we do not give up.

Galatians 6:9 ESV

35

God blesses those who patiently endure testing and temptation. Afterward they will receive the crown of life that God has promised to those who love Him.

James 1:12 NLT

36

There has never been the
slightest doubt in my mind that
the God who started this great
work in you would keep at it and
bring it to a flourishing finish.

Philippians 1:6 THE MESSAGE

37

"I will refresh the weary
and satisfy the faint."

Jeremiah 31:25 NIV

38

Be truly glad. There is wonderful joy
ahead, even though you have
to endure many trials for a little while.

1 Peter 1:6 NLT

39

People with their minds set on You,
You keep completely whole, steady
on their feet, because they keep
at it and don't quit. Depend on
GOD and keep at it because in the
LORD GOD you have a sure thing.

Isaiah 26:3-4 THE MESSAGE

40

We rejoice in our sufferings, because
we know that suffering produces
perseverance; perseverance, character;
and character, hope. And hope does
not disappoint us.

Romans 5:3-5 NIV

*Though our feelings
come and go, God's love
for us does not.*

C. S. Lewis

Is this Really My Life?
God's Love

41

Nothing in all creation will ever be able
to separate us from the love of God.

Romans 8:39 NLT

42

God's love is meteoric, His loyalty
astronomic, His purpose titanic, His
verdicts oceanic. Yet in His largeness
nothing gets lost; not a man, not
a mouse, slips through the cracks.

Psalm 36:5-6 THE MESSAGE

43

"I lavish unfailing love for
a thousand generations on those
who love Me and obey My commands."

Deuteronomy 5:10 NLT

44

"When you come looking for Me, you'll find Me. Yes, when you get serious about finding Me and want it more than anything else, I'll make sure you won't be disappointed. I'll turn things around for you."

Jeremiah 29:13-14 THE MESSAGE

45

May you experience the love of Christ, though it is too great to understand fully. Then you will be made complete with all the fullness of life and power that comes from God.

Ephesians 3:19 NLT

46

How blessed is God! Long before
He laid down earth's foundations,
He had us in mind, had settled on us
as the focus of His love, to be made
whole and holy by His love.

Ephesians 1:3-5 THE MESSAGE

47

The LORD says, "I will rescue those
who love Me. I will protect those
who trust in My name."

Psalm 91:14 NLT

48

You are a chosen people. You are royal
priests, a holy nation, God's very own
possession. He called you out of the
darkness into His wonderful light.

1 Peter 2:9 NLT

When the world says,
"Give up,"
Hope whispers,
"Try it one more time."

Anonymous

Is this Really My Life?
Hope

49

The LORD is good to those
whose hope is in Him.

Lamentations 3:25 NIV

50

May the God of hope fill you up
with joy, fill you up with peace, so
that your believing lives, filled with the
life-giving energy of the Holy Spirit,
will brim over with hope!

Romans 15:13 THE MESSAGE

51

We rejoice in the hope of the
glory of God. And hope does not
disappoint us, because God has poured
out His love into our hearts by the
Holy Spirit, whom He has given us.

Romans 5:2, 5 NIV

52

There is surely a future hope for you,
and your hope will not be cut off.

Proverbs 23:18 NIV

53

Hope deferred makes the heart sick,
but a desire fulfilled is a tree of life.

Proverbs 13:12 ESV

54

I wait for the LORD, my soul waits,
and in His word I put my hope.

Psalm 130:5 NIV

55

No one whose hope is in God
will ever be put to shame.

Psalm 25:3 NIV

56

Let us hold tightly without wavering
to the hope we affirm, for God can be
trusted to keep His promise.

Hebrews 10:23 NLT

*If you lose hope, somehow you lose
the vitality that keeps life moving,
you lose that courage to be,
that quality that helps you go
on in spite of it all.*

Martin Luther King, Jr.

Let me tell you the secret
that has led me to my goal.
My strength lies solely
in my tenacity.

Louis Pasteur

Is this Really My Life?
Strength

57

I can do everything through Him
who gives me strength.

Philippians 4:13 NIV

58

The LORD is my strength and
shield from every danger. I trust
Him with all my heart.

Psalm 28:7 NLT

59

Those who hope in the LORD
will renew their strength. They will
soar on wings like eagles; they will
run and not grow weary, they will
walk and not be faint.

Isaiah 40:31 NIV

60

The LORD gives His people strength.
The LORD blesses them with peace.

Psalm 29:11 NLT

61

"Do not fear, for I am with you;
do not be dismayed, for I am your God.
I will strengthen you and help you;
I will uphold you with My
righteous right hand."

Isaiah 41:10 NIV

62

God is our refuge and strength,
a very present help in trouble.

Psalm 46:1 ESV

63

"In repentance and rest is your
salvation, in quietness and trust
is your strength."

Isaiah 30:15 NIV

64

She sets about her work vigorously;
her arms are strong for her tasks.

Proverbs 31:17 NIV

*Of all the rights
of women, the greatest is
to be a mother.*

Anonymous

Mom-on-the-Go

Loving Being a Mom

*Look at a day when you
are supremely satisfied at
the end. It's not a day when
you lounge around doing
nothing; it's when you've
had everything to do,
and you've done it.*

Margaret Thatcher

Mom-on-the-Go
Fulfillment

65

"I know the plans I have for you,"
declares the LORD, "plans to prosper
you and not to harm you, plans to
give you hope and a future."

Jeremiah 29:11 NIV

66

The LORD called me before
my birth; from within the womb
He called me by name.

Isaiah 49:1 NLT

67

The LORD will fulfill His purpose
for me; Your steadfast love, O LORD,
endures forever. Do not forsake
the work of Your hands.

Psalm 138:8 ESV

68

"I came to give life – life in
all its fullness."

John 10:10 NCV

69

I have learned in whatever situation I
am to be content. I can do all things
through Him who strengthens me.

Philippians 4:11, 13 ESV

70

I will be glad and rejoice in
Your unfailing love, for You have seen
my troubles, and You care about
the anguish of my soul.

Psalm 31:7 NLT

71

The LORD is my shepherd,
I shall not be in want.

Psalm 23:1 NIV

72

An appetite for good brings
much satisfaction.

Proverbs 13:25 THE MESSAGE

*God could not be
everywhere and therefore
He made mothers.*

Jewish Proverb

73

Her children arise and call her blessed;
her husband also, and he praises her.

Proverbs 31:28 NIV

74

Nothing gives me greater joy
than to hear that my children are
following the way of truth.

3 John 4 NCV

75

"Don't get worked up about what may
or may not happen tomorrow. God will
help you deal with whatever hard things
come up when the time comes."

Matthew 6:34 THE MESSAGE

76

Children are a gift from the LORD;
babies are a reward.

Psalm 127:3 NCV

77

Grandchildren are the crowning
glory of the aged; parents are
the pride of their children.

Proverbs 17:6 NLT

78

Be content with who you are, and don't
put on airs. God's strong hand is on you;
He'll promote you at the right time.
Live carefree before God; He is most
careful with you.

1 Peter 5:6 THE MESSAGE

*Children are
the anchors that
hold a mother
to life.*

*Maternal love
is a miraculous substance
that God multiplies
as He divides it.*

Victor Hugo

The Fabric of a Mother

What Makes You a Mother?

*A faithful friend
is an image of God.*

French Proverb

The Fabric of a Mother
Friends

79

"Where two or three are gathered in My
name, there am I among them."

Matthew 18:20 ESV

80

Join the company of good
men and women, keep your feet
on the tried-and-true paths.

Proverbs 2:20 THE MESSAGE

81

"I give you a new command:
Love each other. You must love each
other as I have loved you. All people will
know that you are My followers
if you love each other."

John 13:34-35 NCV

82

The one who blesses others is
abundantly blessed; those who
help others are helped.

Proverbs 11:25 THE MESSAGE

83

You use steel to sharpen steel,
and one friend sharpens another.

Proverbs 27:17 THE MESSAGE

84

Friends come and friends go, but
a true friend sticks by you like family.

Proverbs 18:24 THE MESSAGE

85

The heartfelt counsel of a friend is as
sweet as perfume and incense.

Proverbs 27:9 NLT

A true friend is one who knows all about you and likes you anyway.

Christi Mary Warner

*A woman who treasures,
respects and honors
her husband is a Queen
in his eyes.*

Anonymous

86

Find a good spouse, you find a good
life – and even more: the favor of GOD!

Proverbs 18:22 THE MESSAGE

87

A wife of noble character is her
husband's crown, but a disgraceful
wife is like decay in his bones.

Proverbs 12:4 NIV

88

A wife is bound to her husband
as long as he lives.

1 Corinthians 7:39 NLT

89

Wives, submit to your own husbands, as to the Lord. For the husband is the head of the wife.

Ephesians 5:22 ESV

90

A wife must respect her husband.

Ephesians 5:33 NCV

91

Love each other with genuine affection, and take delight in honoring each other.

Romans 12:10 NLT

*A perfect wife is one
who doesn't expect
a perfect husband.*

Anonymous

*The soul is healed
by being with children.*

Fyodor Dostoevsky

Kids

92

"Let the little children come to Me, and do not hinder them, for the kingdom of heaven belongs to such as these."

Matthew 19:14 NIV

93

"Whoever embraces one of these children as I do embraces Me, and far more than Me – God who sent Me."

Mark 9:36-37 THE MESSAGE

94

I prayed for this child, and the LORD has granted me what I asked of Him. So now I give him to the LORD. For his whole life he will be given over to the LORD.

1 Samuel 1:27-28 NIV

95

"Can a woman forget the baby she nurses? Can she feel no kindness for the child to which she gave birth?"

Isaiah 49:15 NCV

96

The LORD says, "As surely as I live, your children will be like jewels that a bride wears proudly."

Isaiah 49:18 NCV

*While we try to teach
our children all about life,
our children teach us
what life is all about.*

Angela Schwindt

*One good mother is worth
a hundred schoolmasters.*

George Herbert

Motherly Duties

Be the Best Mom
That You Can Be

*Children need
models more than
they need critics.*

Joseph Joubert

Motherly Duties
Be a Loving Example

97

The ways of right-living people glow
with light; the longer they live,
the brighter they shine.

Proverbs 4:18 THE MESSAGE

98

Don't lose sight of common sense
and discernment. Hang on to them,
for they will refresh your soul.

Proverbs 3:21-22 NLT

99

In every way be an example of doing
good deeds. When you teach, do it
with honesty and seriousness.

Titus 2:7 NCV

100

The LORD approves of those who are good.

Proverbs 12:2 NLT

101

Wise living gets rewarded with honor; stupid living gets the booby prize.

Proverbs 3:35 THE MESSAGE

102

Hate what is wrong. Hold tightly to what is good.

Romans 12:9 NLT

103

Do everything in love.

1 Corinthians 16:14 NIV

104

She speaks with wisdom, and faithful instruction is on her tongue.

Proverbs 31:26 NIV

105

Trouble chases sinners, while blessings reward the righteous.

Proverbs 13:21 NLT

Be as patient with others as God has been with you.

Anonymous

Motherly Duties

Have Patience

106

I waited patiently for the LORD; He inclined to me and heard my cry.

Psalm 40:1 ESV

107

If you suffer for doing good and endure it patiently, God is pleased with you.

1 Peter 2:20 NLT

108

We continue to shout our praise even when we're hemmed in with troubles, because we know how troubles can develop passionate patience in us, and how that patience in turn forges the tempered steel of virtue, keeping us alert for whatever God will do next.

Romans 5:3-4 THE MESSAGE

109

Be still before the Lord and wait
patiently for Him. Those who wait
for the Lord shall inherit the land.

Psalm 37:7, 9 ESV

110

God proves to be good to the
one who diligently seeks. It's a
good thing to quietly hope, quietly
hope for help from God.

Lamentations 3:25-26 THE MESSAGE

111

Be patient in tribulation,
be constant in prayer.

Romans 12:12 ESV

112

May the Lord direct your hearts
to the love of God and to the
steadfastness of Christ.

2 Thessalonians 3:5 ESV

113

The longer we wait, the more
joyful our expectancy.

Romans 8:25 THE MESSAGE

*There are two
lasting bequests we
can give our children.
One is roots.
The other is wings.*

Hodding Carter, Jr.

Motherly Duties

Raise Godly Kids

114

Train a child in the way
he should go, and when he is old
he will not turn from it.

Proverbs 22:6 NIV

115

My child, listen to me and do as I say,
and you will have a long, good life. I will
teach you wisdom's ways and lead you
in straight paths.

Proverbs 4:10-11 NLT

116

My child, pay attention to my words;
listen closely to what I say. Don't ever
forget my words; keep them
always in mind. They are the key to life
for those who find them; they bring
health to the whole body.

Proverbs 4:20-22 NCV

117

Do not exasperate your children;
instead, bring them up in the training
and instruction of the Lord.

Ephesians 6:4 NIV

118

We can see who God's children are:
Those who do not do what is right are
not God's children, and those who do
not love their brothers and sisters
are not God's children.

1 John 3:10 NCV

119

All Scripture is inspired by God and
is useful to teach us what is true. It
corrects us when we are wrong and
teaches us to do what is right.

2 Timothy 3:16 NLT

120

If you do not punish your children, you don't love them, but if you love your children, you will correct them.

Proverbs 13:24 NCV

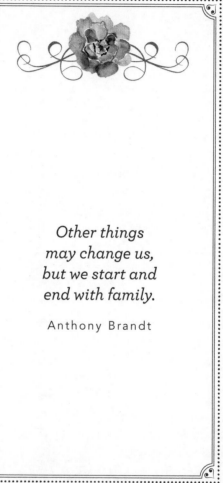

*Other things
may change us,
but we start and
end with family.*

Anthony Brandt

Motherly Duties
Serve Your Family

121

"If you try to hang on to your life,
you will lose it. But if you give up your
life for My sake, you will save it."

Matthew 16:25 NLT

122

"Now that I, your Lord and Teacher,
have washed your feet, you also should
wash one another's feet."

John 13:14 NIV

123

God loves a cheerful giver. And
God is able to provide you with every
blessing in abundance, so that having all
sufficiency in all things at all times, you
may abound in every good work.

2 Corinthians 9:7-8 ESV

124

"Whoever wants to be great among you
must serve the rest like a servant.
In the same way, the Son of Man did
not come to be served. He came
to serve others and to give His life
as a ransom for many people."

Matthew 20:26, 28 NCV

125

"Give, and you will receive.
Your gift will return to you in full.
The amount you give will determine
the amount you get back."

Luke 6:38 NLT

126

Love always looks for the best, never
looks back, but keeps going to the end.

1 Corinthians 13:7 THE MESSAGE

Motherly Duties
Try Conflict Resolution

127

"Love your neighbor as yourself."

Matthew 19:19 ESV

128

Do not let the sun go down
while you are still angry.

Ephesians 4:26 NIV

129

Control your temper, for anger
labels you a fool.

Ecclesiastes 7:9 NLT

130

A gentle answer will calm a
person's anger, but an unkind answer
will cause more anger.

Proverbs 15:1 NCV

131

Love one another deeply,
from the heart.

1 Peter 1:22 NIV

132

If anyone slaps you on one cheek,
offer him the other cheek, too.

Luke 6:29 NCV

133

Do everything in love.

1 Corinthians 16:14 NIV

134

Cast all your anxiety on Him
because He cares for you.

1 Peter 5:7 NIV

Peace reigns
where our Lord reigns.

Julian of Norwich

*The love of God is broader
than the measures
of man's mind; and the
heart of the Eternal is most
wonderfully kind.*

F. W. Faber

Time-Outs

Godly Help
to Cope with Crises

*To pray is to mount on
eagle's wings above the clouds
and get into the clear heaven
where God dwells.*

Charles H. Spurgeon

Time-Outs

Prayer

135

The eyes of the Lord are on
the righteous, and His ears are
open to their prayer.

1 Peter 3:12 ESV

136

Pray for each other. The earnest
prayer of a righteous person has
great power and produces
wonderful results.

James 5:16 NLT

137

Give attention to Your servant's
prayer, O LORD my God. Hear the cry
and the prayer that Your servant is
praying in Your presence.

2 Chronicles 6:19 NIV

138

"Whatever you ask for in prayer,
believe that you have received it,
and it will be yours."

Mark 11:24 NIV

139

God's there, listening for all who pray,
for all who pray and mean it.

Psalm 145:18 THE MESSAGE

140

"Call upon Me in the day of
trouble; I will deliver you,
and you will honor Me."

Psalm 50:15 NIV

141

God's Spirit is right alongside
helping us along. If we don't know
how or what to pray, it doesn't
matter. He does our praying in and
for us, making prayer out of our
wordless sighs, our aching groans.
He knows us far better than
we know ourselves and keeps
us present before God.

Romans 8:26-27 THE MESSAGE

142

In the morning, O LORD,
You hear my voice; in the morning
I lay my requests before You
and wait in expectation.

Psalm 5:3 NIV

You have made us for Yourself, and our heart cannot be stilled until it finds rest in You.

St. Augustine

Time-Outs

Rest

143

The LORD is my shepherd, I shall not be
in want. He makes me lie down in green
pastures, He leads me beside quiet
waters, He restores my soul.

Psalm 23:1-3 NIV

144

"Come to Me, all who labor and are
heavy laden, and I will give you rest.
You will find rest for your souls."

Matthew 11:28-29 ESV

145

"My people will live in peaceful
places and in safe homes and
in calm places of rest."

Isaiah 32:18 NCV

146

"On the seventh day God
rested from all His work."

Hebrews 4:4 NIV

147

Don't you know God enjoys giving
rest to those He loves?

Psalm 127:2 THE MESSAGE

148

I can lie down and go to sleep,
and I will wake up again, because
the LORD gives me strength.

Psalm 3:5 NCV

Time-Outs
Time with God

149

I love Your clear-cut revelation.
You're my place of quiet retreat;
I wait for Your Word to renew me.

Psalm 119:113-114 THE MESSAGE

150

"Live in Me. Make your home in Me.
If you make yourselves at home with
Me and My words are at home in you,
you can be sure that whatever you ask
will be listened to and acted upon."

John 15:4, 7 THE MESSAGE

151

"It takes more than bread to
stay alive. It takes a steady stream
of words from God's mouth."

Matthew 4:4 THE MESSAGE

152

The Lord is with you while
you are with Him. If you seek Him,
He will be found by you.

2 Chronicles 15:2 ESV

153

I pray to God – my life a prayer – and
wait for what He'll say and do. My life's
on the line before God, my Lord,
waiting and watching till morning.

Psalm 130:5-6 THE MESSAGE

154

Let us draw near to God, with a sincere
heart in full assurance of faith.

Hebrews 10:22 NIV

155

As a deer pants for flowing streams,
so pants my soul for You, O God. My
soul thirsts for God, for the living God.
When shall I come and appear
before God?

Psalm 42:1-2 ESV

156

Your words are my joy and
my heart's delight.

Jeremiah 15:16 NLT

157

The Word of the LORD is right and true;
He is faithful in all He does.

Psalm 33:4 NIV

*I need nothing
but God, and to lose
myself in the heart
of Jesus.*

Margaret Mary Alacoque

Family Life

Scripture on Matters
of the Heart

Seek God first in all you do – then His light will shine on the road you should take.

Anonymous

Family Life
Guidance

158

The LORD says, "I will guide you along the best pathway for your life. I will advise you and watch over you."

Psalm 32:8 NLT

159

"Call to Me and I will answer you, and will tell you great and hidden things that you have not known."

Jeremiah 33:3 ESV

160

We do not have a High Priest who is unable to sympathize with our weaknesses. Let us then with confidence draw near to the throne of grace, that we may receive mercy and find grace to help in time of need.

Hebrews 4:15-16 ESV

161

The LORD directs the steps
of the godly. He delights in
every detail of their lives.

Psalm 37:23 NLT

162

Show me the right path, O LORD;
point out the road for me to follow.

Psalm 25:4 NLT

163

The LORD will guide you always.

Isaiah 58:11 NIV

164

"I know His commands lead
toeternal life; so I say whatever
theFather tells Me to say."

John 12:50 NLT

Family Life
Health

165

"I will give you back your health and heal
your wounds," says the LORD.

Jeremiah 30:17 NLT

166

He was wounded for the wrong we did;
He was crushed for the evil we did.
The punishment, which made us well,
was given to Him, and we are
healed because of His wounds.

Isaiah 53:5 NCV

167

"The sun of righteousness will
dawn on those who honor My name,
healing radiating from its wings.
You will be bursting with energy."

Malachi 4:3 THE MESSAGE

168

"I am the Lord who heals you."

Exodus 15:26 NCV

169

Those who look to Him for help
will be radiant with joy; no shadow
of shame will darken their faces.

Psalm 34:5 NLT

*When wealth is lost, nothing
is lost; when health is lost,
something is lost; when
character is lost, all is lost.*

Billy Graham

If you have health,
you will probably be happy,
and if you have health
and happiness, you have
all the wealth you need,
even if it is not
all you want.

Elbert Hubbard

*Be the mate God
designed you to be.*

Anthony T. Evans

Family Life
Marriage

170

Most important of all, continue to
show deep love for each other, for
love covers a multitude of sins.

1 Peter 4:8 NLT

171

Be sure to stop being angry
before the end of the day.

Ephesians 4:26 NCV

172

May the patience and encouragement
that come from God allow you to
live in harmony with each other the
way Christ Jesus wants. Then you
will be joined together, and
you will give glory to God.

Romans 15:5-6 NCV

173

Love is patient and kind. It is not irritable, and it keeps no record of being wronged. Love never gives up, never loses faith, is always hopeful, and endures through every circumstance.

1 Corinthians 13:4-5, 7 NLT

174

Give honor to marriage, and remain faithful to one another in marriage.

Hebrews 13:4 NLT

175

May the Lord make you increase and abound in love for one another.

1 Thessalonians 3:12 ESV

176

The Christian wife brings
holiness to her marriage, and
the Christian husband brings
holiness to his marriage.

1 Corinthians 7:14 NLT

Trust God to provide all your needs – He has a never-ending supply of resources at His disposal, and He loves to share.

Anonymous

177

God will use His wonderful
riches in Christ Jesus to give you
everything you need.

Philippians 4:19 NCV

178

"If God cares so wonderfully for
wildflowers that are here today and
thrown into the fire tomorrow, He will
certainly care for you. Seek the
Kingdom of God above all else, and
live righteously, and He will give
you everything you need."

Matthew 6:30, 33 NLT

179

Submit to God and be at peace
with Him; in this way prosperity
will come to you.

Job 22:21 NIV

180

"Bring the whole tithe into the storehouse, that there may be food in My house. Test Me in this," says the LORD Almighty, "and see if I will not throw open the floodgates of heaven and pour out so much blessing that you will not have room enough for it."

Malachi 3:10 NIV

181

The LORD is my chosen portion and my cup; You hold my lot. The lines have fallen for me in pleasant places; I have a beautiful inheritance.

Psalm 16:5-6 ESV

182

Honor God with everything
you own; give Him the first and the
best. Your barns will burst, your
wine vats will brim over.

Proverbs 3:9-10 THE MESSAGE

If you want to feel rich,
just count all the things you have
that money can't buy.

Anonymous

*True wisdom is
gazing at God.*

Isaac the Syrian

Family Life
Wisdom

183

If you need wisdom, ask our generous God, and He will give it to you. He will not rebuke you for asking.

James 1:5 NLT

184

Wisdom will multiply your days and add years to your life.

Proverbs 9:11 NLT

185

If you call out for insight and raise your voice for understanding, if you seek it like silver and search for it as for hidden treasures, then you will find the knowledge of God.

Proverbs 2:3-5 ESV

186

Wisdom is sweet to your soul. If you find it, you will have a bright future, and your hopes will not be cut short.

Proverbs 24:14 NLT

187

Real wisdom, God's wisdom, begins with a holy life and is characterized by getting along with others. It is gentle and reasonable, overflowing with mercy and blessings.

James 3:17 THE MESSAGE

188

"I will give you a wise and discerning heart, so that there will never have been anyone like you."

1 Kings 3:12 NIV

*We are made wise not by
the recollection of our past,
but by the responsibility
for our future.*

George Bernard Shaw

*The family was
ordained by God before
He established any other
institution, even before He
established the church.*

Billy Graham

We Are Family

Scripture for Making You
a Strong Family Unit

The goal of every married couple, indeed, every Christian home, should be to make Christ the Head, the Counselor and the Guide.

Paul Sadler

We Are Family
A Godly Home

189

As for me and my household,
we will serve the LORD.

Joshua 24:15 NIV

190

Jesus replied, "All who love Me
will do what I say. My Father will love
them, and We will come and make
Our home with each of them."

John 14:23 NLT

191

Don't for a minute let this Book
of The Revelation be out of mind.
Ponder and meditate on it day and
night, making sure you practice
everything written in it.

Joshua 1:8 THE MESSAGE

Godly Home

192

"I will be a father to you, and you
shall be sons and daughters to Me,"
says the Lord Almighty.

2 Corinthians 6:18 ESV

193

Bow in prayer before the Father
from whom every family in heaven
and on earth gets its true name.

Ephesians 3:14-15 NCV

194

I look up to the mountains –
does my help come from there?
My help comes from the LORD,
who made heaven and earth!

Psalm 121:1-2 NLT

All the wealth in the world cannot be compared with the happiness of living together happily united.

Margaret of Youville

*If we focus on differences
our focus is on each other.
If we focus with unity,
our focus is on God.*

Anonymous

We Are Family
Unity

195

Be of one mind, live in peace.
And the God of love and
peace will be with you.

2 Corinthians 13:11 NIV

196

There are different kinds of service,
but the same Lord.

1 Corinthians 12:5 NIV

197

"I in them and You in Me.
May they be brought to complete
unity to let the world know that You
sent Me and have loved them even
as You have loved Me."

John 17:23 NIV

198

It is good and pleasant when
God's people live together in peace!
There the LORD gives His blessing
of life forever.

Psalm 133:1, 3 NCV

199

You are joined together with peace
through the Spirit, so make every effort
to continue together in this way.

Ephesians 4:3 NCV

*Everyone has inside them
a piece of good news.
The good news is you don't
know how great you can be!
How much you can love!
What you can accomplish!
And what your potential is!*

Anne Frank